cover design: Skip Moen

CROSSING

The Struggle for Identity

Skip Moen

"Every family is really a great, transgenerational story. It's a story of all the many individuals involved, of their personal struggles, their ways of interacting and expressing emotion, of their ways of loving, of arguing, of communicating and more."

Patrick Carnes, Debra Laaser, Mark Laaser – *Open Hearts: Renewing Relationships With Recovery, Romance & Reality*, p. 8.

The stories in the Hebrew Bible are not exactly history. That is to say, they are not records of chronological events as we would recount them for the evening news. Hebrew stories are more like instructions to the director of a film, the bare outline of the plot begging to be filled in with lighting, sound, sub-plots, actors' personalities and the dozens of other things that make a storyline into a movie. Biblical stories might have happened, but how they happened and what effect they had on the people involved are elements often left to the reader. The real story is found between the lines. After all, these were once oral accounts, passed from one generation to another by those who added the intonation, the body language and the occasional knowing wink that made them fascinating. Today we read them as someone else's history, not our own ancestry. Today we pay attention to the *text* and ignore the unwritten *context*. As a result, the real dynamics of the stories are often overlooked. We move on without asking how these events shaped the lives of men and women struggling to understand the faithfulness of God.

The story of Jacob at the brook Jabbok is one of these truncated, mysterious accounts—an account that cries out to be read between the lines. So that's what we will attempt to do. In the following pages, we will speculate, meditate, ruminate and concentrate on the hints, innuendo and unwritten assumptions that fill in the bare plot in order to understand how God interacts with His people, then and now. Some of our exploration may seem to stretch the limits of "proper" exegesis, but, then, this is a story—and stories need scenery to become real. So let's add some scenery and see what we learn.

Skip Moen
Montverde, FL
Christmas 2015

Acknowledgements

This book is the result of conversations with Luzette Wessels and Mariaan van Staden. Sharing thoughts with these two ladies in South Africa led me to look deeper into the story of Jacob. I was also blessed by discussions with Zelda Pollard who offered key insights into family dynamics.

Amanda Youngblood and Cyndee Sullivan provided invaluable proofreading and suggestions that give the work greater clarity and readability.

Thank you, one and all.

1.

Dark. Water rushing over the feet. Up to his knees now. He carries his cloak wadding through the stream. Cold. Catches a glimmer on the surface from the thumbnail moon. No lights. No fires. No candles. Dark. Really dark. The walls of the ravine close out the stars. The deep shadows hide something. Climbs the bank to the sand. Wet. Shivering.

He's alone. All the others are over there, on the other side. Safe. But not here. Not on this side in the dark. Something is coming. Just a faint sound above the rush of the water. It draws closer. A shape. Upright. A man? Before he can put on his cloak, the shape is nearly upon him.

Where did he come from? Why is he here? Who is he? A quick glance across the river. No, nothing has changed. They are still there. Suddenly the shape rushes at him. Too late to even speak. The man is striking the first blow. He sees the eyes, fierce, determined, terrifying. Yellow, like a demon.

Another blow. Defend. The third hits his arms. He strikes back. Feels the impact on muscle. The thud of connection. The man doesn't drop. Strike again. Wildly. No aim. Just push away. But the arms are around his neck. Powerful. The arms of a trained combatant. He smells the breath of the aggressor. Slips free. Caught again. A blow to the head, then the chest, then the head. He staggers but counters. Kick. Strike. Clutching to get inside the attack. Down to the ground.

The sand on the bank grinds his face. His mouth fills with the grit. With all his strength, he pushes up. Spits out the coppery taste of blood. The man is on him again. Wrestling. Sweat, blood. A grip like the jaws of a lion. Down again. Up. Over backwards.

Each move anticipated. Each blow countered. Each feint equaled. Who? Who is this? Heavy breathing. Gasping for air but still he comes. Clothes thrown on the sand. A grip on the shirt. Tears. Another blow to the side. Rib bruised. Cheek cut. He lands two punches. The man staggers, then charges. Both on the ground, rolling, clawing. No retreat.

Why? Why is he attacking? Not the one I expected. I know that one. He would fight differently. This one has animal ferocity. He wants to kill.

One hour. Two hours. Both bloodied. Body to body. Knees and elbows skinned. Faces cut. Blood in the beards. Wrestling. Wrestling. But there is no submission, no retreat. Groans. No words. No time for words. Attack. Attack. Attack.

His legs are knocked out from under him. The man is on top, pressing against his chest, hands to the neck. Counter with an elbow to the face. The man is knocked loose. Get up! Now! Rush him. A step and then the man's knee comes up, strikes the groin. Flashes of light in his eyes as he falls. He can't get up. His legs are done. The man stands over him. The kill is coming. A fatal blow to a fallen enemy.

He grips the man's leg with all the strength he has left.

2.

This story begins long before that night of battle. Long before he was born. This story begins with Abraham.

Abraham was a man of obedience. When God called him out of Ur, Abraham went. He did not question. He did not argue. He went. Obedience came first—and last. Abraham's life is marked by two great acts of unquestioning faithfulness. The first act was God's call to leave his homeland and go to a place God would show him. The second act was the request to offer Isaac. Once again, God makes His desire known and Abraham does not hesitate.

"Abraham!" And he said, "Here I am." The Hebrew response is *hinneni*, literally, "Behold, me!" Abraham's response is the echo of Adam's denial. The Lord asks Adam, "Where are you?" The interrogative does not imply physical location. It is about *expectation*. *'ay-yekka* is not, "Where are you hiding?" Rather, it is, "Why are you not here where you are expected to be?" Adam is not present to YHVH, but Abraham is. Abraham's *hinneni* is the basic exclamation of willingness. It is the exclamation that I stand ready to do the will of the Lord. "Father, behold *me*! I am willing to serve at your request. I am ready to do anything you ask. Look at me, your humble servant."

The spirit of *hinneni* is quite the opposite of the religious world. It is the spirit of humility, of the

11

recognition that I am His only because of *Him*, not because of anything I have done or will do. *Hinneh* (Behold) simply acknowledges that God is the *one and only Sovereign* of our fellowship and He alone chooses whom He will call. *Hinneni* is my personal expression of complete obedience, not to a creed or a doctrine or a dogma, but to a Master who has the supreme right to assign tasks according to *His* plans and purposes.

Abraham begins with *hinneni* and ends with *hinneni*, but in between life gets in the way. He acts to protect himself at the expense of his wife. He discounts the promise of YHVH in his acquiescence to Sarah's suggestion about Hagar. He abandons his first-born son in order to reduce marital conflict. He perpetrates half-truths when they are convenient. Of course, there are moments of intense spiritual recognition and daring: the rescue of Lot, the plea for Sodom, the tithe to Melchizedek. Abraham—a man of great beginnings and great endings—with a life of up and down in the middle.

Then there is Isaac. The Genesis account contains a very odd expression about YHVH's relationship with Isaac. In Genesis 31:42, the patriarchs' connection with YHVH is described as "the God of Abraham, the dread of Isaac." The Hebrew word for Isaac's relationship to YHVH is unique. This is the only place in Torah where a patriarch's connection with YHVH is described like this. The word is *paḥad*, a word that means, "fearing with emphasis either on the immediacy of the object of fear or upon the resulting trembling. The verb may refer to the kind of fear aroused by a *paḥad* 'terror'."[1]

Rabbi Ismar Schorsch's commentary on this unusual description is incredibly important.

> Isaac never seems to recover from his binding at the hands of his father. Abraham may have passed the divine test at Moriah, but Isaac's religious growth is permanently stunted. In a mystifying omission, the Torah reports after the aborted sacrifice that only "Abraham then returned to his servants (Genesis 22:19)." On the way to Moriah, the Torah states on two separate occasions that father and son walked together, as if to stress their unity of purpose (Gen. 22:6, 8). Yet once the ordeal is over, the Torah omits to tell us that Isaac accompanied his father home. Did he flee from the scene in terror and incredulity? It is the kind of narrative gap that begs for reader participation.
>
> Curiously, we are told later that the name by which God was known to Isaac is "the Fear of Isaac," a name of God not found elsewhere in the Torah (Gen. 31:42). Does the nomenclature suggest that Isaac knew God only as a demonic presence, a source of dread, as God surely must have appeared to him at Moriah?

---

[1] Bowling, A. (1999). 1756 פָּחַד. In R. L. Harris, G. L. Archer, Jr. & B. K. Waltke (Eds.), *Theological Wordbook of the Old Testament* (R. L. Harris, G. L. Archer, Jr. & B. K. Waltke, Ed.) (electronic ed.) (720). Chicago: Moody Press.

The Torah offers only the most fragmentary data about Isaac, which are all strikingly bereft of spirituality. Indeed, they point to a man who, having faced death early, lusted for life ever after.[2]

Perhaps Schorsch's insight is another example of the psychological impact parents have on their children. Isaac's subsequent favoritism toward Esau may be a result of his father's apparent lack of concern for his son's life. Certainly Isaac ignores YHVH's design for the younger of his twins, although there are hints that Isaac regretted his behavior, as we shall see. Nevertheless, "neither Abraham nor Isaac nor Jacob are portrayed by the Torah as men without flaws, or saints who could do no wrong. They exhibit the warts and weaknesses we recognize in ourselves. What sets them apart, rather, is the nobility and courage of their convictions as evinced in moments of luminous insight and supreme self-denial."[3]

Jacob is not merely the individual self-made man. No one really is despite the Western cultural emphasis on individualism. Jacob is Hebrew and in Hebrew thought Jacob is the product of the experience of his grandfather and his father, and, of course, the wives of these men. When Jacob encounters the man on the wrong side of Jabbok, he is not alone. The psychological presence of the men in his genealogy is there with him. How they are there is the subject of this investigation.

---

[2] Ismar Schorsch, Chancellor's Parashah Commentary, November 13, 1993.
[3] Ibid.

Isaac's life seems to have been tragically altered by the experience of Moriah. Any young man would probably have felt the same way if his father attempted to offer him as a sacrifice. Abandonment, confusion, peril, rejection—we can only imagine how this experience may have affected Isaac and, more importantly, Isaac's relationship to God. It is not much of a stretch to conclude that Isaac felt God Himself was untrustworthy, unreliable and uncaring. Is it any wonder that Isaac's relationship is characterized by *paḥad*?

One other factor plays a role in the spiritual development of Abraham's son. It is confusion about the meaning of love. Why doesn't Abraham offer *himself* as the sacrifice rather than Isaac? Wouldn't any father who truly loved his son do just that? This is the patriarch who is courageous enough to stand before YHVH and argue for the life of Lot, a nephew. This is the man who negotiates with YHVH over a city that certainly deserved punishment. This is the father who grieves over sending Ismael into the wilderness. Yet he makes no protest at all when it comes to his beloved son, Isaac. What must Isaac have thought about the "love" of his father when he witnessed such callous behavior in the name of devotion to YHVH? Is there any doubt that Isaac's relationship with his father and with his father's God would be affected? What does "love" mean when such lack of compassion for a son's life is manifest? Isaac shows favor to Esau because Esau is full of life. Esau is free of spiritual doubts. He is empty of obligations to the terrifying God of the past. Esau simply lives—the kind of naïve existence that Isaac may have wished belonged to him.

But parents also have regrets. Somewhere in the subconscious, Isaac must have wrestled with YHVH's actions as sovereign. He knew that his father Abraham was devoted to this God and his life was spared by God's hand. He knew that God had blessed him with wealth and power. He knew that God chose Jacob, not Esau. Despite his parental preference for Esau, perhaps *because of it*, there was the submerged awareness that God was active in the lives of his two sons, each according to divine purposes. If we consider the dynamics of Isaac's critical encounter with Jacob, we may find hints of parental remorse for his preferential treatment and spiritual denial.

Nevertheless, something happened to Isaac. The father who was willing to argue with YHVH to prevent the destruction of a thoroughly evil city was unwilling to argue with YHVH for the life of his only beloved son. In fact, YHVH doesn't *command* Abraham to sacrifice Isaac. The text of Genesis 22:2 should be translated, "He said, 'Now take, *please* (*na*), your son, your only son, whom you love, Isaac, and go to the land of Moriah, and offer him there as a burnt offering on one of the mountains of which I will tell you.'" The Hebrew contains the particle *na* attached to the verb translated "take." This addition, often overlooked in translation, changes the verb from a command to a request. [4]

Each time *na* is used in God's speech to a man, God asks that man to do something that defies reason.

---

[4] http://skipmoen.com/2009/03/05/the-hidden-please/

The first three occasions involve the promise to Abraham. The last two involve Moses and Isaiah. In every example, the use of *na* indicates that God is fully aware that He is asking the person to do something that is completely contradictory to reason. And this is the secret of the hidden *please*. In the speeches of God, *na* is an announcement that God's ways are not our ways and His thoughts are not our thoughts. Amazingly, God recognizes this very fact and He *condescends* to our inferiority by asking us to *please, if we don't mind too much*, follow His instructions since they come from His sovereign control of the universe. The crucial point with regard to Isaac is that God *doesn't demand* the sacrifice, yet Abraham willingly accepts the request. What incredible impact this must have had on Isaac, the son who was to be offered. His father is willing to fight over ten righteous men in Sodom but not willing to offer any resistance about his own son. Isaac is more than confused. He is traumatized. Rejected, treated as worthless, abandoned, perhaps even despised. What other conclusion can he draw? How can he go back to the former days when his own father fails to love him? What kind of God must this be who would ask such a thing? And what kind of father is so devoted to the terrifying God that he would *willingly* comply? Isaac is the product of Moriah and as the product of Moriah, he passes his trauma to his sons.

3.

To understand what really happened means reading between the lines. "Rebekah was listening while Isaac spoke to his son Esau. So when Esau went to the field to hunt for game to bring home, Rebekah said to her son Jacob, . . ." (Genesis 27:5-6). We think we know the story. Jacob receives the blessing that Isaac intended for Esau. The patriarchal tradition is broken. Hatred between the brothers grows. Under pretense, Jacob flees for his life. Decades later he returns—and wrestles in the dark with a stranger on the riverbank. As Jacob begins the journey toward reconciliation, he encounters an enemy that can't be beaten. It all seems to start with Isaac's mistaken blessing. But if we carefully examine the blessing event, we may discover that Isaac is doing much more than being duped by his wife and younger son.

The first clue comes in the unexplainable narrative declaration, "When Isaac was old and his eyes were too dim to see." The narrator offers this justification for Isaac's decision to give the paternal blessing. But the story of Isaac continues for many decades after this event. According to the text, Isaac dies at the age of one hundred and eighty. Traditionally, the blessing inadvertently given to Jacob occurs when Isaac was one hundred and twenty-three. That means he lived another fifty-seven years after the day he told Esau that he was concerned about his death. This clue suggests that perhaps Isaac was aware of the dysfunctional family dynamics (what man wouldn't be?) and intentionally arranged the opportunity in order to provide some reconciliation.

The blindness of which the Torah speaks in Isaac's old age, which allows Jacob, at Rebekah's instigation, to steal Esau's blessing, is therefore not just a physical infirmity of old age, but also a lifelong aversion to matters spiritual (Gen. 27:1). Rashi agrees that this condition goes back to his experience on the altar. As he lay there awaiting his fate, the heavens parted and the angels beheld the ghostly sight. The tears they shed in anguish fell on Isaac's eyes and dulled his vision for life. Rashi's comment, I think, is intended to explain the permanent damage done to Isaac by his father's religious zeal. For the rest of his life he chose to make his home in the temporal realm. True to his name, Yitzhak ("he shall laugh") wanted to enjoy life.[5]

Secondly, Jacob and Esau were sixty-three on that fateful day. For sixty-three years Isaac knew the sight, smell, sound and actions of his son. Are we to conclude that because of failing *eyesight* Isaac did not know the difference between Jacob and Esau? What father could be so naïve? In fact, the story suggests that Isaac was aware of the duplicity. He remarked about the speed of the kill, the sound of the voice, the touch of the skin. And, instructively, when he proclaims he will eat and offer the blessing, he does not say, "I will eat of my son Esau's game." He leaves out the name of the son. Could it be that after sixty-three years of favoritism and a refusal to accept the will of YHVH

---

[5] www.jtsa.edu/prebuilt/ParashahArchives/5754/toldot.shtml

20

in the matter, Isaac is coming to terms with God's true intention? John Parson's comment on the *two* blessings offered by Isaac is important:

> Jacob actually received *two* blessings from his father. The *first* blessing—given to a *disguised* Jacob—focused on material blessings: The "dew of the heaven," the "fatness of the earth," "plenty of grain and wine," political power and hegemony (Gen. 27:28-29), whereas the *second* blessing— given to an *undisguised* Jacob—focused on his role as God's chosen patriarch of Israel (Gen. 28:3-4). The difference between these blessings turned on Isaac's restored vision. His first blessing was tailored to the character of Esau as his "natural choice," whereas his second blessing looked beyond mere appearances to behold the vision that was originally given to his father Abraham.[6]

Why would Isaac give the *second* blessing if he actually felt deceived? Perhaps Isaac recovered his spiritual awareness and constructed an event that would allow him, without apologizing, to re-establish what he knew to be God's agenda. Isn't Isaac's action in the second blessing really an admission and an attempted reconciliation? Sometimes it just isn't possible to actually say, "I'm sorry." Sometimes we simply arrange things so that we can make up for our mistakes without ever admitting that we were mistaken. This is especially

---

[6] John Parsons, Hebrew4Christians, http://www.hebrew4christians.com/Scripture/Parashah/Summaries/Toldot/Two_Blessings/two_blessings.html

true when one of the mistakes is to not trust God. " . . . although other people in our lives appear to be the source of our unresolved emotional issues, they are simply external mirrors of our inner experiences. We project our relationships with ourselves onto others. These unresolved emotions are usually primary factors that keep us from being fully present in our relationships."[7]

Abraham was devoted. He began in obedience. He ended in obedience. But his son, Isaac, is the "in-between man," the man who withdraws from a God he does not understand, a God he dreads because one day, long ago, his father told him that God wanted a sacrifice that would end his life. Isaac withdraws into the comfort of his wife, the security of his wealth and the stability of a life without religious commitment. Isaac withdraws from his God of *paḥad* because such a God is a being to fear. Much better to simply leave all those feelings alone. Bury them beneath the contingencies of life. Retreat to trivialities. Eat, drink, have children, look for comfort and escape. Except, of course, that we can't leave this fear alone. No matter how hard we try to escape what happened to us when we were forming our view of the world, the specter of the past haunts us. We do to our children what was done to us. Abraham was willing to sacrifice Isaac at God's request. Isaac sacrificed God's desire for Jacob by denying Jacob's priority until one day he could no longer live with the complications. One

[7] J. Steenkamp, *SHIP: Spontaneous Healing Intrasystemic Process: The Age-Old Art of Facilitating Healing,* JO Steenkamp (Pretoria, South Africa) 2002, p. 75.

day Isaac realized that he would have to contend with the God of *paḥad* and do what he should have done years before—honor YHVH's intention.

And Jacob? What happens to Jacob in this dysfunctional, anti-spiritual family dynamic? When the father withdraws from God out of fear, the son learns that God cannot be trusted. That means a new creed is formed. "At all costs, take care of yourself." What gain you have in life is up to you. Be savvy. Be smart. No one is coming to your rescue. There is no God watching out for you.

4.

". . . consoling himself concerning you by planning to kill you."[8] Rebekah spirits Jacob away from danger with another manufactured emotion. She knows her husband very well. Plant one more fear in his mind and he will react defensively. Let Isaac think he is in charge. Jacob's teacher in subterfuge and duplicity has no equal. But what was Esau really thinking? How is murder in the heart any form of consolation?

The Hebrew text is *mitnāḥem lehorgeka*. The NASB translates, "consoling himself concerning you by planning to kill you," but the text literally reads, "comforts himself by-to slaughter you." The translation must *add* "planning" in order to fit our syntactic expectation. But it isn't *planning* that comforts Esau. It is the present mental enactment of violence. Esau lives out the act as if it were happening. He isn't scheming to murder. In his thought, he is murdering Jacob *now*! And the thought is delicious. He turns it over and over in his mind. The exquisite pleasure of revenge. The flavor of seeing his enemy's blood soak the ground. This is another form of the hunt. He feels the tautness of the bowstring. He hears the whistle of the arrow, the sound of impact and the scream of fright as his enemy realizes that life will soon be drawn away. How enthralling it is! In his mind, Jacob lies dead at his feet. Sweet revenge. Oh, how sweet the smell of his blood! "The greatest cause of

---

[8] Genesis 27:42 NASB

distress in humankind lies in the act of comparison, which is the root of conditional acceptance."[9]

There is little doubt Esau is capable. Rebekah knows her other son far too well to suppose his anger will cool. But should we expect anything less? Esau is victimized by clever manipulation. He is humiliated. He is cheated. Why would a man's man respond differently? Relief from anger requires violence toward the offender. It is the way of the world. It is the way of a world without compassion, without grace, without forgiveness—that is to say, without God. The son of a father who has withdrawn from God is a son who lives in a world where strength is the only useful commodity. Enemies must be eliminated. The powerful are duty-bound to destroy those who victimize. Jacob must die!

There is another motive between the lines. It is deeper than revenge.

When you were a child, you learned how to process emotions by reacting to the world around you. This isn't an explicitly cognitive process. You don't *think* about it. You simply respond to perceived reality. If you are humiliated, you create defensive mechanisms. This might be withdrawal or its opposite—attention-seeking behaviors. You expect the world to care for you, to protect you, to value you. Parents provide the mechanisms that frame a child's worldview and when they do not protect or

---

[9] Steenkamp, *Op. cit.*, p. 5.

care or value, children often internalize those forms of abuse by drawing the conclusion that they are not good enough to be protected or cared for or valued. In a world where adults are final authority figures, children have no choice but to assume that deprivation of basic psychological essentials is their fault. As a result, they grow up to be men and women without balanced emotional health. In other words, they become dysfunctional adults.

Some degree of emotional trauma is part of every childhood environment. After all, growth occurs in system imbalance. No pain—no gain. But there is an extremely fine line between positive emotional resolution and dysfunctional reaction. For men who believe that conflicts are settled by violence, the world is a very threatening place. Children who grow up believing that conflict is resolved by force didn't begin that way. They were taught, by word, deed and example, that subjugation is resolution. And they learn those lessons from parents.

Isaac is a man afraid of what God might do. He is a man who dreads spiritual involvement. He is a man who learns to live by his own strength. After his father returned from Mount Moriah, the text tells us that Abraham lived in Beersheba. But when we next read of Isaac, the text tells us Isaac came from Beer-lahai-roi, a place in the Negev. The name means, "Well of the living one who sees me." It is of some consequence that this is the same place where Hagar encountered God after fleeing from Sarah. In other words, Isaac does *not* live with his father. He lives in the place of the mother of his rival step-brother, Ishmael. Isaac, son of the promise, lives apart from the man who received the promise. He lives with the one who was not included. Perhaps in spite of the fact that he carried the promise, he lived apart from it. Perhaps more than anything else, Isaac needs to be "seen." As defense against the trauma of parental sacrifice, Isaac feels that the God of Abraham does not truly see him. The God of his father sees only the sacrifice, not the person. So he runs to the place where there is a God who does see.[10]

And Isaac has a son. Actually, two sons. The only time we hear of Isaac pleading with God is on behalf of his wife for sons. God answers him with two boys, but even this is conflict and struggle. Rebekah's statement about the struggle is revealing.

"If it is so, then why am I this way?" (Genesis 25:22).

We tend to read the question instead of the conditional introduction. "If it is so." If *what* is so? What is it that Rebekah acknowledges as the precondition to the struggle she feels? The Hebrew is *'im-ken*, literally, "if thus." Rebekah asks why these two unborn children seem to be fighting in the womb. Unlike modern women, she does not ask for information about her pregnancy. She accepts the fact of the struggle. She just wants to know *why*!

---

[10] Luzette Wessels (in private correspondence) points out that the place of Abraham's sacrifice, *Moriah*, may be understood as "God will see" (from Midrah Tanchuma). The irony is that this is the place where God sees Abraham's faithfulness and the place where Isaac feels he is not seen.

Consider the circumstances again. Rebekah cannot get pregnant. Her husband prays to a God that he would just as soon avoid. But he knows that God has the power of life and death, and he asks for life. God grants his request. Rebekah conceives. But the result is not what she or Isaac expected. The result is conflict, turmoil and inter-uterine warfare. God answered. There is no doubt about that. But *why* would God answer this way? What did she do to deserve this? What did her husband do to cause her this pain? It is instructive that Rebekah inquires, not Isaac. Rebekah is willing to confront God and ask, "Yes, You caused this to happen, but why? Why is it so difficult?" Rebekah is the one who intercedes, like her father-in-law, Abraham. Isaac remains outside the conflict. He has no intention of engaging God any more than is absolutely necessary.

How often have we experienced the same confusion? We believe God answers prayer so we pray for the resolution of our traumatic situations. And God answers—but not the way we wanted Him to. His answer comes with arrangements, implications and expectations that we did not anticipate or desire. Now we are stuck. Now we have to accommodate divine intervention and come to terms with His purposes. Rebekah's query is our complaint. "Why did you do this, Lord?" The answer, of course, is that it isn't about us. It is about the eternal purposes of YHVH and we are but bit players in that divine drama. Our preoccupation with an egocentric universe is shattered in the answer we receive. God is there, but it is His game, not ours.

Two sons are born. Isaac's prayer is answered. But one is favored. The one who is favored is also the one who lives apart from the promise. Isaac turns away from the God whose promise came through the hands of a father who was willing to slaughter him. He turns toward those who feel abandoned and rejected. Certainly he knows that Esau is the rejected one. So Isaac chooses him, a replay of his own struggle with the God of his father. And he inadvertently perpetrates the same emotional trauma on his own son, the rejected one. Ultimately Isaac does the same thing with Esau that he experienced with his own father. He rejects him. When Esau experiences the betrayal of his brother, he walks over the same ground that his father experienced at the hands of the devoted grandfather.

Esau must have heard the story. "Father, tell me about my grandfather again. Tell me how it all happened. Tell me why we live so far from where he was." What story does Isaac tell? The story of his own traumatic experience? The story of the grandfather's God, the God he does not trust? What picture of the world does his son receive? "God can't be trusted. God shows favorites. God is powerful and terrifying." This is a world devoid of compassion, mercy and trust. The sins of the father show up in the lives of the children. Already primed for disappointment, Esau is trained to react, to secure his immediate future by physical means. To hunt and kill.

Beneath revenge is loss. In Esau it is the loss of the greater character of God, a loss that results from a father who did not know mercy and who ran from involvement. Beneath revenge is the loss of a life greater than immediate need, the loss of generational perspective, the loss of divine purpose. Beneath revenge is a man who never knew the intimate generosity and compassion of YHVH. Esau carries the emptiness of rejection. And just like Cain, rejection means someone else is to blame.

When does Isaac decide to bless the son who is not of the promise? When he is afraid (*pahad* again) that he will no longer "see." How will he atone for those years of running from the promise, the promise that almost killed him, the promise from a God who does not "see" him? He will force God to see—to see the son who is not accepted. He will circumvent the will of the God who did not see him. He will require God to see because he will give the blessing to the one *he* sees. He will not look on the son whom God chose. Why would he? To look on that son is to subject him to the same risk. The promise comes laced with death. Better by far to reconstruct the promise so that it is controllable than to place his other son in the hands of a God who might one day say, "Please take your son."

Beneath Esau's revenge is the desire to be valued, not as an escape from the father's terrifying God but simply for himself, for the man he has made himself to be. As we noted, "the greatest cause of distress in humankind lies in the act of comparison, which is the root of conditional acceptance."[11] A child who grows up in a household without a loving God will adopt whatever picture of God he finds in his

---

[11] Steenkamp, *Op. cit.*, p. 5.

parents. [12] Esau found fear in his father and scheming in his mother. Esau found favoritism, unequal evaluation and worth and the need to please. Esau found a God who was part of a murky past, not a present reality. Why give away the birthright? Because all that really mattered to this man was the *immediate*. Because there was no instruction about the greater purposes of God. Because this man never knew the gentle touch of a God who loved him for just being alive.

Revenge is the result of a warped picture of God. Since Esau grew up with the bent images of God, it is hardly surprising that he finds fault in his brother and is more than willing to kill him in order to settle the score. Esau's God would certainly do the same, wouldn't He? After all, Esau's God nearly had his father killed for no apparent reason than proof of "love", whatever that might mean when you are ready to kill your son.

In the end, Esau is a man of self-pity. Self-pity means that I don't get what I believe I am entitled to have—and that means someone else is responsible for my loss. This is the root of anger and the source of revenge. Perhaps he learned this medicating behavior from his father, a man who apparently felt that he had to run from God to survive. Isaac favored Esau because Esau was a man of immediacy, a man whose life was governed by today's needs and today's pleasures. Isaac experienced life differently. But Esau's lust for life was balanced on a razor's edge. It could become

---

[12] For an examination of how Sarah contributed to this dysfunctional family and her impact on Isaac, see http://skipmoen.com/2007/03/04/sarah---a-life-of-discontent/

the motivation for spectacular engagement, for noble deeds and amazing accomplishments. But it could also become the justification for blind entitlement, anger and blame. How did the son of Abraham respond to God's inescapable purposes? With glorious involvement or with the trauma of *paḥad*? Isn't the son made in the father's image?

Once in Isaac's life God seemed to be a tyrant, a God with blood-lust. Isaac ran from that God. But there was another event. During the time of famine, YHVH appeared to Isaac (Genesis 26) with a message of hope and blessing. How does Isaac respond to the uninitiated encounter?

"Do not go down to Egypt; stay in the land of which I shall tell you. Sojourn in this land and I will be with you and bless you, for to you and to your descendants I will give all these lands, and I will establish the oath which I swore to your father Abraham. I will multiply your descendants as the stars of heaven, and will give your descendants all these lands; and by your descendants all the nations of the earth shall be blessed; because Abraham obeyed Me and kept My charge, My commandments, My statutes and My laws."[13]

What can we discern from this promise? First, notice that God's blessing to Isaac is *not* based on Isaac's faithfulness. In fact, Isaac's interaction and relationship with YHVH isn't even mentioned. Isaac is the beneficiary of someone else's devotion, namely, his father Abraham, the same father that put him on the altar. Secondly, YHVH's promise

---

[13] Genesis 26:2-4 NASB

reiterates the exemplary obedience of Abraham, an obedience that created a turning-point trauma in Isaac's life. It is as if God said, "Look, Isaac. What your father Abraham did was right. I was honored in his decision. Yes, your life was at risk, but that doesn't matter. Now I will bless you because your father did what I asked."

Is that comforting? Does that make up for the traumatic event? Is it now swept under the carpet because God will *reward* Isaac? Where is the Isaac who stands up before God and shouts, "Why did You do that to *me*? Don't You know what happened to me? Don't You care that I spent my life in fear of You? Do You think that now that You promise *material reward* I can somehow pretend that it had no effect on me?"

The text is illuminating. "So Isaac lived in Gerar." There is *no* comment about Isaac's relationship with God. There is no mention of his devotion or obedience. There is only the bare fact that he *complied*! He did what he was told. Yes, God blessed him. He became wealthy and powerful. But there is never any mention of engagement with God, of worship, fidelity or dedication. Even when others acknowledge that God is with him, Isaac's personal allegiance to YHVH goes unnoticed.

Esau lives the life of disregard for obligations, traditions and expectations. Perhaps it is the life Isaac wanted, a life of escape from a God who asked too much.

5.

Isaac's life is one of spiritual weakness. In the face of God, Isaac wilts. He is powerless. He doesn't argue. He doesn't protest. He doesn't debate. He is not his father Abraham. What does Isaac do? He runs! But in his son Esau, Isaac finds vicarious power. The power to act as his own man, to be victorious over enemies. To fight back! Esau is Isaac as Isaac wished to be.

It's not surprising that he marries a woman who also believes in power. Not the power of men. Not spears and swords and physical combat, but another kind of power—the power to manipulate. The power to stand before God and argue. The power of purpose. Rebekah is a woman who knows her own mind, a woman connected to something greater than herself, just as her father-in-law was connected to a purpose greater than himself. Isaac sees in his wife something he must have admired in his father but could not come to believe about himself—the power to obey and to *question* God.

Schorsch's comment is helpful.

> But the real hero of this ancestral saga is Rebekah, who displays an unfailing religious sensibility throughout. Her quick acceptance of the invitation to marry Isaac from a total stranger bespeaks a full awareness of God's hand in the remarkable events at the well (Gen. 24:58). In the midst of a difficult pregnancy, with twins in her womb, she turns to inquire of God herself,

36

without benefit of any intermediary (Gen. 25:22). And Rebekah rises to protect Jacob because she alone senses that religious leadership in the family ought not to be the exclusive prerogative of the first-born son. Her advocacy marks a brave first step toward opening the ranks of religious leadership to all who are religiously qualified.[14]

Schorsch's conclusion that "the divinely guided history of Abraham's clan is predetermined and quite indifferent to individual virtue or suffering," reflects Isaac's conclusion. God's purposes are *fait accompli*. You might as well live as best you can since there is nothing you can do about what God does. But this isn't Rebekah! Rebekah determines that if her husband will not align himself with God's greater purposes, then *she* will make sure the eternal plan happens. She knows Jacob is the chosen one. Surely she communicated this to her husband. But he seems determined to avoid God's calling. So she seizes the opportunity to force it. Rebekah is Sarah without Hagar. Her method is deception, not temptation.

Sarah knew the purpose of God. In her zeal to see God's promise fulfilled, she determined to *assist* the plan by creating a human solution to a divine problem. Hagar, the fruit offered to Abraham, was simply the means for Sarah to attain what God promised *without God*. The pattern set in motion by Havvah is repeated by Sarah and passed to Rebekah. God needs help. Strong women are called to act.

---

[14]www.jtsa.edu/prebuilt/ParashahArchives/5754/toldot.shtml

The *'ezer kenegdo*[15] is designed to direct a husband in the path God chooses. The line between God's way and another way to reach the same end is a delicate one, as Havvah discovered. But the temptation is always there. The *'ezer kenedgo* sees what God wants. The *'ezer kenegdo* is designed to know how to accomplish that end. But the path is always lined with the temptations of human solutions instead of trust in YHVH. For a woman who knows what to do, the detour appears to be a sure way to reach the objective.

Rebekah knows Jacob is the one, so she determines to make sure Jacob receives the blessing. We often view Rebekah's instructions as deceit and conspiracy, but that overlooks the conviction that God's hand will be served in her actions. From Rebekah's point of view, Isaac is about to undo what God wants done. How should she respond? Is it reasonable to suggest she should confront Isaac, insist that he alter his intention and align himself with God's choice? She has lived with the man for decades—decades of spiritual avoidance and vicarious power. Does she have any grounds for believing that he will, at this apparently last moment, alter his life choice? The fact that his *second* blessing hints at some spiritual reconciliation is not in play here. Rebekah follows what she believes God desires. Her only "sin" is avoiding confrontation with her entrenched husband. Perhaps we can find that one excusable.

---

[15] *'ezer kenegdo* is the Hebrew phrase used by YHVH to describe the design and role of the woman in Genesis 2. It is a role of power, spiritual sensitivity and guidance. I have explored and elaborated this role in my book, *Guardian Angel* (2010).

Of course, this part of the story forces us into an ethical dilemma. Should we lie to accomplish God's will? Should we deceive in order to fulfill His desire? Perhaps our Western ethical categories are not sufficient to capture the ambiguity that surrounds Semitic spirituality. We want an absolute ethics, one that gives us precise behavioral directions. We want an ethical code that relieves us of personal responsibility. But the truth is that life comes in all kinds of colors and gray is one of the predominant ones. It is often virtually impossible to tell what to do *when it is time to do something*. The fact that the story does not condemn Rebekah, or even Jacob, is some indication that there is a lot more flexibility in the fuzzy math of Semitic observance. Today's world pushes us toward insistence on certainty, but perhaps that is simply a reaction to the fear and shame we have ingested in a world distinctly devoid of the awareness of God. Perhaps we *need* to be certain so that we can justify our actions instead of feeling our relationships. A therapist might encourage Rebekah to engage her husband in early childhood trauma resolution. A counselor might discuss alternatives to deceit. But in the moment of crisis, when it looks like the eternal plan will be put at risk, human beings tend to take the eternal burden on themselves and act in God's place. We might question Rebekah and Jacob in *hindsight*, but it is more than likely that we would have done the same. Therapy is usually an *after-the-fact* analysis.

Rebekah is the spiritual head of this home. She listens to the Lord despite the spiritual vacuum in her husband. Are we to condemn her for this? Or are we encouraged to see a woman who uses her strength to construct a solution to a very pressing concern? What does the *'ezer kenegdo* do when her man refuses the clear calling of God? We might be inclined to treat Rebekah with some degree of equivocation. We don't want to endorse her duplicity but it is obvious that God used her actions to further His plans. That leaves us in a quandary— right where we are supposed to be. Answers to life's real tensions are not always black and white.

6.

"Is he not rightfully named Jacob?"[16] Esau feels betrayed. But God's hand was against him, not Jacob's. Jacob simply acted a part that had to happen in some way, at some time. The blessing, "Be master over your brothers, and may your mother's son bow down to you," could never have been given to Esau. Jacob is rightly named, not because he is the deceiver but because God Himself orchestrated the authority of the younger. We might not like the way that the scene plays out, but behind the curtain is YHVH and the actors appear to do nothing more than follow His direction even when they improvise.

The translation "Is he not rightfully named" is a gloss for *hakiy qara shem*, literally, "if when to call a name." That is to say, according to Esau when Jacob was called by the name he bears, his character was determined. In Hebrew thought, a person lives up to his name. Now Jacob has once again demonstrated that he is what he was called. But this implies much more than the name "Jacob." Our contemporary view of names has little connection to the biblical idea of naming. Names in the Bible are often designations of the inner person, a sort of shorthand way of describing the total personality and behavior of the person. Jacob, of course, is *not* the Hebrew name. The name is *Ya'akob*, a word derived from the verb *'aqab*, meaning, "to take by the heel, to supplant." TWOT notes that the noun *'aqeb* can be used for anything at the rear, and is

---

[16] Genesis 27:36 NASB

42

used by David (Psalm 49:5) to describe those who lie in wait to ambush (Psalm 41:9). In Christian Messianic prophecy, this is the word used in Genesis 3:15 ("strike the heel"). The name Ya'ako<u>b</u> plays a crucial part in the story of wrestling on the edge of the brook Jabbok (which is also an important name).

But Ya'ako<u>b</u> doesn't necessarily mean "supplanter" or "deceiver." In fact, it is Esau who provides the connection between Ya'ako<u>b</u> and the verb 'aqab. The verse is actually a play on words. Esau says, "He is rightfully called Ya'ako<u>b</u> because he has ya'qe<u>be</u> me." Esau connects the name to the act of deception. The only meaning attached to the name prior to Esau's designation is "the one at the rear, the one who comes after." But this "one who came after" had already been designated as the one who will have authority.

Esau's complaint gives a double meaning for his brother's name. It is not simply the name that matters. In this case, the name is also a description of the action. It is as if Esau is saying, "When he was named, doesn't that name fit him, 'the deceiver – Ya'ako<u>b</u>.'?" Both name and character are summarized in the single word, according to Esau.

Once again we are confronted with the interplay between the divine sovereignty and human intervention. Is Ya'akob's action really deception? Does God ever condemn the subterfuge? Or is it the human path of divine election? Could the blessing that Isaac determines to give to the wrong son have been circumvented in some other way? Or does Isaac, after a lifetime of favoring the child he knows is not God's elect, actually set up the circumstances so that he can do the right thing without repentance? Does he foreshadow an action that Ya'ako<u>b</u> will take decades later when he reverses the blessings of the sons of Joseph?

By contrast, Esau is a name derived from the primary root, *asah*, "to do, to make." The root itself has a very wide range of meanings, everything from "accomplish" to "bruise."[17] Esau is, in almost every respect, the man his father is not. He is characterized by direct action, immediate and sometimes without consideration of consequence. Esau is a man of passion, of unrestrained *yetzer ha'ra*.

Isaac must certainly recognize that such a man cannot fulfill the greater plan of God. The two sons actually represent the duality of Isaac's soul. One is the desire to fulfill what God intends, to play out the role of the chosen one and accomplish the eternal purposes of YHVH. Ya'ako<u>b</u> may play his part through cunning but he acts according to the prophetic word of YHVH given before his birth. He obeys the spiritual head of the household, his mother, Rebekah. Esau, on the other hand, represents the opposite pole of Isaac's consciousness, the man who *acts*, the man who is not apathetic or passive in life.

Esau is Isaac without God consciousness. Giving away the birthright is the consequence and symbolic representation of a man who has no need of God or tradition. Isaac must know this since Esau's

---

[17] See Strong's list #H6213

44

complaint clearly implies the forfeiture of birthright was common knowledge. What must a father think of a son who so easily gives away a promised blessing? This is a father who is the path of the promise and whose past experience with his own father demonstrates the crucial importance of the promise. What must he think of a son who shows no care for the greater plan? But this is also Isaac's struggle. In fact, YHVH blesses Isaac *after* Moriah. We have examined that blessing. It cements the commitment of YHVH to Isaac as *a part of* a greater divine plan. Certainly Isaac is aware of this. Gentiles confirm God's handiwork in Isaac's life. But for sixty-three years Isaac has turned away from that greater divine plan.

This means that Isaac is a man in excruciating tension. Shall he deny what God has done and circumvent God's plan? Is his arrangement for the blessing of his son actually a final act of disobedience? Or is it the artful construction of an opportunity to repent without admission of guilt?

Esau is caught in a web not of his own making. He is caught in a web constructed by his father and his father's God. He certainly plays a role, but the design of the web was put in place before he was born, and just like Ya'ako<u>b</u>, he is a pawn in a much bigger chess game. Without recognition of the sovereignty of YHVH, Esau views all the actions of the players as treachery, but the story is much bigger than his self-pity and anger. Abraham, Isaac and Ya'ako<u>b</u> are tied together because of the choices of YHVH and Esau is collateral damage. The simple story is not so simple.

7.

"And they brought grief to Isaac and Rebekah."[18] No family story can be complete without the influence of those brought into the family. In this story, we know the names of Esau's first two wives, Judith and Basemath. We also know that they were Hittites. The son who follows his father by withdrawing from YHVH brings new tension into the family. He looks for comfort and satisfaction *outside* the clan. Are we to imagine that this was a surprise, that Esau showed up one day and announced, "Oh, by the way, I've married two Hittite women"? Not likely. Marriages were *family* contracts in the ancient Near East. They involved significant arrangements, especially when the groom's family was powerful and wealthy. Marriages were made on the basis of political, social and economic benefits. That means things probably started well. But in time, ah, well you know the rest of the sentence. In time, Isaac and Rebekah felt *morah*.

The word *morah* means bitterness and sorrow. The text says more than "brought grief." The construction is the verb *haya* plus the noun *morah*. We might understand it as "and life becomes bitter." The verb is an imperfect. The action is continuous. Over time it becomes clear to Isaac and Rebekah that these two women are the source of on-going agony, bitterness and sorrow. A big mistake. One that cannot be undone.

---

[18] Genesis 26:35 NASB

Victor Hamilton notes, "Hebrews expressed tragic, unpleasant experiences in terms of the sense of taste, the bitter."[19] Judith and Basemath leave a bad taste in the mouths of Isaac and Rebekah. But the reason for this foul taste is Esau, not the women. It is Esau who brings them into the family. Esau might be quite content with these two wives. They might satisfy him, but they are distasteful to the parents. Rebekah uses this bitter taste to justify sending Ya'ako<u>b</u> away. The text makes it abundantly clear that Isaac was concerned about drinking more vinegar with the potential wife of his second son. What must the father think when his favored son causes him such distress? Yes, Isaac apparently endorses the man of action, the vicarious exemplar of his repressed desire to be free of obligation, but he also knows what it means to have the comfort of a woman chosen by God. Rebekah comes at a time when Isaac needs solace, not only from the death of his mother but also from his perception of a dysfunctional family. Esau, on the other hand, acts without regard to the will of YHVH. Isaac might have secretly wished that he had the strength to stand up against the divine hand, but when that reality takes hold of the family, Isaac sees, unfortunately too late, what a disaster it is to choose without divine awareness.

Even this experience of bitterness (*morah*) is a repetition of past family dynamics. Both Abraham and Sarah know *morah*. Sarah experiences *morah*

---

[19] Hamilton, V. P. (1999). 1248 מָרַר. In R. L. Harris, G. L. Archer, Jr. & B. K. Waltke (Eds.), *Theological Wordbook of the Old Testament* (R. L. Harris, G. L. Archer, Jr. & B. K. Waltke, Ed.) (electronic ed.) (528). Chicago: Moody Press.

over Hagar and her son, rivals for Abraham's affection and potential threats to inheritance. What does Sarah do? She commands her husband, "Drive out this maid and her son."[20] Her bitterness pushes her to kill her enemy. And what is Abraham's reaction? The text says he was "greatly distressed." Do you suppose there was no bitterness toward his wife? What does Isaac experience in all this? A child seeks comfort somewhere, but where does he go when his father and mother are at odds, when his childhood brother and second mother are gone, when all he hears are arguments, all he feels is tension? The suitcase of emotions fills up. He carries it with him for the rest of his life. Now we understand the broader meaning of Isaac's marriage: "thus Isaac was comforted after his mother's death."[21] But it was much more than his mother who died.

Isaac found comfort, but he did not find resolution. He causes the same tension in his family that characterized his childhood, and the result is the same: *morah*.

Put yourself in Isaac's place during those last formative years. Your father, Abraham, talks of the promise of YHVH. But there is the disconnection between his talk and the actions taken by your mother and her handmaid. You grow up with a boy who is your father's first born, but whose very presence brings *morah* to your mother. You hear the arguments, experience the taunting, know the

---

[20] Genesis 21:10 NASB
[21] Genesis 24:67 NASB

sorrow and the anger. In the end, that boy you played with is gone—and his mother with him. Your father is distraught. Your mother relieved. Where are your loyalties? How do you interpret caring when your father sends away a young boy and his mother to die? What does bitterness mean to you if you grow up in a household where it is a daily reality?

Isaac wants nothing to do with that kind of life, but his son's choice brings it all back. The outsider is back inside, only now twice as present. What does the boy/man Isaac discover? All those feelings of confusion, of broken love relationships, of years of bitter arguments, of rejection and hatred come pouring out once again. This is more than grief. This is a return to childhood agonies never resolved. The only time Scripture speaks of Abraham's love for his wife is at her funeral. Does Isaac remember that? Is love nothing more than struggle between the demands of a wife and the will of God? Isaac, *Yitshāq*, the son who is laughter, probably spent a good deal of time crying. Now his son plays the same game again. This is not simply grief. This is trauma.

Knowing his history, Rebekah easily convinces Isaac that Ya'akob must not be allowed to make the same mistake. Yitshāq ("Laughter") agrees. He has had enough sorrow to last a lifetime. And so he sends away the son whom he knows carries the real promise, not merely to protect the son against the enticement of outside women but to prevent himself from reliving the past once more. Both Rebekah and Isaac resolve issues in the decision. The only one who can't resolve issues is Esau, still playing the role of collateral damage.

Rebekah says to her husband, "I am tired of living because of the daughters of Heth." The translation is far too mild. The verb is *quts*. We must appreciate the emotional power of this word.

> *qûṣ* denotes the deep emotional reaction of the subject issuing in a desired repulsion (or destruction) of the object. Compare the following synonyms: *bā'aš* "to be or become stinking, odious," *gā'al* "to cast away as unclean, to loathe," *šāqaṣ* "to detest as unclean," *tā'ab* "to treat as an abomination" in a ritualistic and, also, a moral and general sense, *dērā'ôn* "object of contempt," and *qûṭ*, a variant spelling of our root. The root occurs nine times.
>
> Understanding the state of mind denoted by this root enlightens many passages. Rebekah complained to Isaac that she loathed her life because of Esau's wives (Gen 27:46). If she is telling the truth perhaps their strange ways had so irritated her that her life had become unbearable. At least this is probably what Isaac believed. It is such an irritation and loathing that is forbidden toward God's fatherly reproof (*qûṣ* is parallel to *mā'as*, q.v.). This word describes God's feelings toward the Canaanites (Lev 20:23) and toward all idolatry (cf. *qûṭ*). Israel used it to describe their feelings toward the manna after prolonged feeding on it (Num 21:5). [22]

---

[22] Coppes, L. J. (1999). 2002 קוּץ. In R. L. Harris, G. L. Archer, Jr. & B. K. Waltke (Eds.), *Theological Wordbook of the Old*

Isaac knows this kind of life. He ran to Beer-lahai-roi to escape *qûṣ*. But childhood traumas often repeat themselves when we are adults if they are not resolved. Esau might be the *vehicle* bringing reminders of childhood trauma into Isaac's life, but he is not the source of that agony. The source is God.

Testament (R. L. Harris, G. L. Archer, Jr. & B. K. Waltke, Ed.) (electronic ed.) (794). Chicago: Moody Press.

8.

"Then Jacob departed." "Then" is the crucial introductory term. Of course, it is only the small addition of a *vav* to the verb *yatsa* ("to go out, to come out, to go forth"). Unfortunately, it is ignored in some translations. Ya'ako<u>b</u> didn't just get up and leave. In fact, in the narrative he didn't leave until Esau took revenge on his parents for the humiliation he felt. The text tells us that Esau saw that Isaac blessed Ya'ako<u>b</u> again, with the second blessing we already examined. Another round of rejection and humiliation. Furthermore, Esau recognized that Isaac instructed Ya'ako<u>b</u> not to marry from the same pool of available women that Esau used. Now Esau sees that his choice of wives is also unacceptable. More humiliation. Round three is the recognition that Ya'ako<u>b</u> obeys his father, demonstrating that both father and son agree on the anticipated plan. It must seem clear to Esau that Isaac is now aligned with Ya'ako<u>b</u>. Both parents appear to reject Esau and choose Ya'ako<u>b</u>. What does Esau do? He ups the ante.

Esau decides that if his father won't accept him and embrace the choices he made for his wives, then he will do what any man's man would do—make his father pay by bringing even more *morah* into his life. "You don't like what I did? After all these years, you side with my *brother*, the deceiver! After all I did to please you, you give up on me just like that? You never really loved me at all, did you? Then I'll show you. I'll do something that will really make you sorry." Self-pitying Esau goes to Ishmael, the rejected brother, and marries Ishmael's daughter.

Consider the family dynamics. Isaac and Ishmael were rivals for their father's attention. In the end, Sarah convinces (is it an ultimatum?) Abraham to abandon Ishmael. Abraham grieves but complies. Now Esau feels abandoned. Who does he go to for consolation? The rejected uncle. But it is not enough to simply receive sympathy from one who has experienced the same fate. Esau also wants revenge, just as he plots revenge against his brother. How does a son get revenge against his father without physically harming him? He acts in way that he knows will cause the father emotional trauma. If Isaac is upset by the women Esau chooses, then Esau will choose one who reminds Isaac of his own psychological turmoil with his father Abraham. Esau will bring a woman back into the household of Isaac who carries the line of the rejected one. Did Isaac think he could forget the strain of the relationship with his half-brother? Not any more. Now Isaac's grandchildren will be constant reminders of his own father's *first* born. Esau twists the knife of Isaac's past as he plunges it into the heart of the man without laughter.

When Isaac fled from the face of God on Moriah, he went to the mother of his half-brother. He found comfort in the household of one who was rejected by the father. His emotional upheaval sought out someone who felt the same chaos. Now Esau looks for the same comfort and returns to the same rejected household. But rather than simply finding comfort, Esau uses this opportunity to drive the wedge deeper. Isaac looked for relief. Esau looks for revenge. How often do we find that the sin of the father escalates when it arrives at the son's doorstep—unless reconciliation arrives first. As C. S. Lewis reminds us, "There is nothing we can do with suffering except to suffer it." Any other behavior is an attempt to reject the pain and control the outcome. Those actions, unfortunately, almost always lead to disconnection with others and with ourselves. "The anger that has no vent in tears makes other organs weep."[23]

Then Ya'akob departs. Whether or not the sequence is temporal or merely a narrative transition doesn't matter. The point of this part of the story is the further emotional damage to the family. It might be that Ya'ako<u>b</u> left immediately, but the story cannot proceed until the reader knows how Esau responds to Isaac's realignment. This gives us another clue to unraveling the mystery of the "dread" of Isaac. While the text doesn't tell us that Isaac finally embraced the God of his father, his actions clearly show us that there has been a change of heart. Isaac comes to terms with the promise and sends forth the one who carries it with his blessing. And he suffers the consequences of all those years of rejecting the sovereignty of God by experiencing even more distance with the estranged first-born son. Every action has a consequence, even those actions we believe are necessary for self-protection. Isaac's avoidance of God's call results in hatred and fear between brothers.

This leads us to the famous passage about "Jacob's ladder." There is some debate about the correct

---

[23] Steenkamp, *Op. cit.*, p. 70.

translation of the Hebrew *sullam*. It might mean something like "stairway" instead of "ladder," but what really matters in this passage is the content of the dream and Ya'ako<u>b</u>'s reaction to the dream. First, we must notice the way YHVH describes Himself in His announcement to Ya'ako<u>b</u>. "I am YHVH, the *elohim* of your father Abraham and the *elohim* of Isaac" (Genesis 28:13). Two things stand out. YHVH treats Ya'ako<u>b</u> as *Abraham's* son. The text does *not* read, "the *elohim* of your grandfather."[24] YHVH designates Ya'ako<u>b</u> as the immediate descendent of Abraham. Why? Could it be that the one who *actively* carries the promise is the primary concern of YHVH? Does YHVH skip Isaac because Isaac failed to embrace the eternal purpose until he was forced to do so by the actions of Ya'ako<u>b</u> and his mother?

We must also notice that, in contrast to Genesis 31:42, YHVH designates Himself as the *elohim* of Isaac. If this is the way God sees His relationship with Isaac, then who describes the same relationship as *paḥad* (dread)? Interestingly, the description "the *paḥad* of Isaac" comes from the mouth of Ya'ako<u>b</u> in a conversation with Laban some twenty years *after* YHVH announces Himself as the *elohim* of Isaac. It is Ya'ako<u>b</u> who views the relationship of his biological father with God as *paḥad* (dread). When we carefully examine Ya'ako<u>b</u>'s statement, we find another oddity. Ya'ako<u>b</u> says, "If the God of my father, the God of Abraham, and the *paḥad* of

---

[24] The Hebrew *'a<u>b</u>* could be translated "forefather" but Isaiah 63:16 describes Israel (Ya'ako<u>b</u>) as the son of YHVH because of the covenantal relationship. The text is ambiguous. My choice of "father" emphasizes the dysfunctional family relationships.

Isaac, had not been for me." The parallelism suggests that Ya'akob may consider himself a son of *Abraham*! The word *'ab* could mean "forefather" or "ancestor," but in this context it seems that Ya'akob is distinguishing between the two progenitors on the basis of their respective relationships with YHVH and he is aligning himself with the relationship of his grandfather rather than his father. This must lead us to ask, "When a son sees the father's relationship with God as one of fear or dread, what kind of message does that communicate?" Does Ya'akob recognize his parallelism with Abraham in God's announcement in the dream and adopt it as a proclamation of his true connection to Abraham rather than Isaac? Once again we are struck with the change in family dynamics brought about by the avoidance behavior of Isaac. When Isaac runs, he takes more with him than his life. He takes the lives of his sons on a journey away from God. In the end, even this son notices that Isaac fears God rather than actively obeying Him. It takes the shock of Rebekah's conspiracy to wake Isaac up to the reality of God's sovereign plan. "What prevents people from being in the now is the endless fantasies which arise from old wounds and the defensive compensations for the wounds."[25] Isaac is now awake, but the patterns he taught his sons still linger.

Ya'akob wakes from the dream saying, "Surely YHVH was in this place and I did not know it." The statement acts as a reminder that YHVH has always been in the life of Ya'akob in spite of the fact that Ya'akob never knew it. The invisible hand

---

[25] Steenkamp, *Op. cit.*, p. 92.

of the Lord has now been revealed. But notice how Ya'ako<u>b</u> responds to YHVH's renewed promise.

"Then Jacob made a vow, saying, 'If God will be with me and will keep me on this journey that I take, and will give me food to eat and garments to wear, and I return to my father's house in safety, then YHVH will be my God" (Genesis 28:20-21). Ya'ako<u>b</u>'s vow is *conditional*. YHVH makes an unconditional promise but Ya'ako<u>b</u> offers his response as a commitment contingent upon a series of physical events. Consider the three-step differences in the patriarchs. Abraham obeys immediately, without conditions. Isaac does not obey in spite of the unconditional promise of YHVH. Ya'ako<u>b</u> accepts the commitment of YHVH but places his own conditions on it. This variation is the context for the combat at the brook. When Ya'ako<u>b</u> returns to the Promised Land, YHVH has fulfilled all the conditions Ya'ako<u>b</u> required. The question is whether Ya'ako<u>b</u> will now fulfill his part of the vow.

This transgenerational dynamic is important. It is the real substance of this story and it is probably the real substance of our stories. When YHVH reveals Himself to Moses, He offers the self-descriptive phrase, *rachum ve-chanoon erech apayim ve-rav chesed ve-emet notzer chesed la'alafim nose avon vafesha ve-chata'ah ve-nake lo yenake poked avon avot al-banim* ("compassionate and gracious, slow to anger, and abounding in lovingkindness and truth; who keeps lovingkindness for thousands, who forgives iniquity, transgression and sin; yet He will by no means leave the guilty unpunished, *visiting*

the iniquity of fathers on the children . . .").[26] We
often think the Hebrew verb *paqad* (not to be
confused with *pahad*) is about God transferring the
sins of the fathers into the lives of their children, but
this is not what the verb means despite the King
James translation. The verb really means that God
oversees the potential damage of the sins of the
fathers, implying that YHVH supervises those sins
so that that they do *not* have their fullest detrimental
impact. Are there consequences? Of course there
are. In this story, the devoted preoccupation of
Abraham traumatizes his son Isaac. That trauma
affects Esau and Ya'ako<u>b</u>, furthering the trauma in
both sons' lives. But it could have been much
worse. Esau could have killed Ya'ako<u>b</u> on the spot.
Isaac could have completely rejected the call of God.
YHVH watched over the situation, and with an
invisible hand, managed the lives of these men and
women so that the eternal purposes were maintained
even if those purposes seemed to take very
divergent paths. We might have written the story
differently, but we aren't the authors, are we?

Our personal stories of trauma, our family dynamics,
have the same effect. We don't see that God is in
this place, perhaps because we are so busy trying to
manage our pain. But God doesn't quit. One day
He reminds us that the promises He made are still in
effect, even if we place more conditions upon them
to protect ourselves from the fear of ruthless trust.
It takes enormous courage (and perhaps some
spiritual push) to let ourselves be tossed about by
the winds of change, but tossed we must be if we
are to experience freedom from those emotional

---

[26] Exodus 34:6-7a

cords that bind us to past trauma. Joe Steenkamp notices that, "We seem to repeatedly attract situations and relationships that resonate perfectly with our most vulnerable feelings, despite our resolutions to avoid them."[27] Such circumstances are *not accidental*. They are indications that YHVH is performing "visitation," that is, He is maneuvering life so that we will come into contact with those silent forces of our past that continue to cause *paḥad*. YHVH does not want us to dread Him but He cannot move us from dread to loving obedience until we have faced the demons we have built within us. Ya'ako<u>b</u> is on the path toward that battle, just as we are, and when he reaches the brook of separation, his demon is waiting.

---

[27] Steenkamp, *Op. cit.*, p. 162.

9.

"Now he arose that same night and took his two wives and his two maids and his eleven children, and crossed the ford of the Jabbok." Genesis 32:22 NASB

Everyone knows the story. Jacob wrestles. He loses. He is blessed. Israel is born. But maybe we know the story too well to actually hear it. Let's start with the geography.

Jabbok, the Hebrew word *Yod-Bet* (doubled)-*Qof*, is an ancient name. That means it was probably written (if at all) in the pictographs of Paleo-Hebrew. Perhaps its origin came from the picture "to make the last household," or "work of the house behind." But notice that the middle radical is doubled. This is a "two house" word. One house is connected with work (*Yod*), the other with what is behind (*Qof*). It is speculation, of course, but the use of the *Bet* is intriguing since it looks both behind and ahead. The future is "behind my head," not visible to me. Could it be that this brook represents both the life Ya'akob will leave behind and the life he cannot yet see in his future? Whatever is happening at this tributary of the Jordan means that one life is ending and another beginning, one household is complete and another proceeds. *Yabboq* is transition, the place where we are emptied before something else can fill us. *Yabboq* is the place of crossing, the border between households, strongholds and ways of living. To cross the *Yabboq* is to cross from past to future, a past that is known even if terrible into a future that is unknown and therefore terrifying.

Notice the story's sequence. At night (an odd time for defensive moves), Ya'ako<u>b</u> removes himself from his family, the last of his "assets" from the days with Laban. He takes his wives and children across the ford. But he returns. Why? Why go back where there is nothing left? The story makes it very clear that "everything else he had" was on the other side of the stream. Does this strategy make any military sense? Ya'ako<u>b</u> leaves himself completely vulnerable, exposed to the impending army of Esau. Furthermore, the stream is not like the Mississippi. It is *small*. Putting his family and possessions on the other side certainly doesn't remove them from danger. It doesn't even remove them from sight. There is no military maneuver here. For some reason, Ya'ako<u>b</u> is impelled to place everything on other side while he returns to the empty side. We need to know why.

The text tells us that he was left alone. The verb is *yatar*—"to remain over, to leave." Derivatives include some things we wouldn't think of: abundance (*yitra*), advantage (*yoter*), excellence (*yitron*) and profit (*motar*). Most of these ideas are connected with excess, that is, what is left over. But this is not Ya'ako<u>b</u>'s definition of the word. His is what remains after everything else is gone. What is that? What is left when everything else is removed? Himself. He remains. He is the left over, the profit of all his labors, the last of what matters to him. What he discovers is what we all discover at the point of emptiness. We are alone.

64

The Hebrew, *lebaddo* does not simply mean "solitude." It carries the sense of being apart, being separated from community and from God. It can mean abandoned, the recognition and emotional trauma of unexpected isolation. Ya'ako<u>b</u> is abandoned, perhaps intentionally so because there is no logical reason for him to retreat to this side of the place where past labor and future household are divided. Perhaps he is compelled to go back across because there is still something unfinished in that place, something non-tangible that cries out to be carried across or be buried on this side. Whatever it is, he must return to face the emptiness of his life. It has all come down to this. In the end, he is alone. All his possessions, all his relationships, evaporate in the dark. It is night—the night when there is nothing left of the former Ya'ako<u>b</u>, the night when it has all moved on—except him.

We must remember that in Hebrew the idea of "man" (*ish*) is *not* about physical being or bodily characteristics. "Man" is a functional term. To be a man is to act in certain ways and have certain relationships. The same ideas are still present today in some African tribes. In one example, to be a man is to be married. Therefore, an *unmarried* male of sixty is a boy while a married male of eighteen is a man. In another example, to be a man is to earn the income for the family. In this case, the seventeen-year-old girl who has a job and brings money to the household is called the "man of the house." In Hebrew, "man" is the designation that summaries all the crucial *relationships* that make up character. For Ya'ako<u>b</u>, his identity as a man is tied to all he possesses, all his family, all his connections to the tribe, his relationship with YHVH, his acceptance and fulfillment of his calling, in other words, his self-identity. And all of that is now on the other side of Jabbok—all except his past.

In that night, in that place, he wrestles. The story isn't clear about his opponent and this ambiguity is crucial to the story. Eventually Ya'ako<u>b</u> believes it to be YHVH, or some representative of YHVH. That doesn't matter nearly as much as the outcome. Ya'ako<u>b</u> is defeated by what is left behind. Of course, there is a sense in which he cannot leave what is left behind *until it defeats him*. It is accumulation of all that has always been his downfall: his maneuvering, his calculation, his self-reliance, his ability to turn mistakes into advantage. In fact, his life has always been about *yatar* (the left over), until now, until *yatar* turns into nothing but the fight.

Let's go down to the ford of Yabboq. No, that's not quite right, is it? You see, *we* can't go there. Only you or I can go there—alone. This is the empty place where you and I are when we are "left over." There is no community here. There is only the last fight with God. What we bring of the life we constructed by ourselves is of no use anymore. That life is done. Here, fighting what is left behind, we are defeated. The result is inevitable even if we prolong the battle. In order to leave this place, we must be blessed—and that blessing does not come without permanent injury. You and I cannot cross Yabboq without a limp.

Someone confronts Jacob in the night; someone who isn't supposed to be there. Or is he? Does Ya'akob go back across the ford of Yabboq because he "knows" (in some Hebraic way) that there is someone he must fight? The text says "a man,"— 'ish—but this isn't any ordinary man. In fact, if the Hebrew word 'ish is understood as it is *used*, not as the lexicons suggest, then this isn't a "man" at all, because 'ish isn't a word for a male human being. 'ish is a word about what makes us self-conscious. Ya'akob wrestles with *identity*, and in the process, he is given a new *identity* summarized in a new name. What comes to Ya'akob, on the wrong side of the Yabboq, a word that means, "the place of pouring out," is his old persona, ready to fight him *'ad alot hashshahar* ("until the breaking of the dawn").

The fear of the coming dawn makes this story even more curious. "Then he said, 'Let me go, for the dawn is breaking' But he said, 'I will not let you go unless you bless me.'"[28]
The phrase translated "until the breaking of the dawn," contains something a bit more mysterious, just as mysterious about the "man" whom Yakob fights. The first two words, *'ad alot*, are not particularly difficult. An adverb and a verb, *'ad alot*, is "as far as" or "until" plus "to ascend, to cause to rise, to lead up." Clearly temporal, the phrase must mean that the fight continued until a time of ascent. But what time is that? The problem is with the noun, *shahar*. Victor Hamilton notes: "A masculine noun generally denoting the breaking of the day, that time just prior to sunrise. Some have

---

[28] Genesis 32:26 NASB

67

taken a clue from the Ras Shamra texts in which *šhr* refers both to the common noun "dawn" and to the name of a deity, Dawn. *Šahar*, along with *šalim*, is born to a woman who has been impregnated by the god El (UT16: Text no. 52). The suggestion is then that there are (veiled) references to this Canaanite deity in the OT [Old Testament], albeit in a demythologized fashion."[29]

Does Ya'akob wrestle with more than a man? Does he wrestle with the remnants of pagan gods, the ones who come at night and fight with men until the ascent of Dawn? Is this perhaps his last battle with the worldview of the household of Laban, a polytheistic community that included YHVH among particular household gods? Or is it an inner struggle like the one in the Garden two millennia later? Does the Messiah repeat the nightlong struggle at Jabbok when he cries out to the Father, "If it is possible, let this cup pass"? Isn't YHVH present in all of these battles? Isn't the sweat of drops of blood a sign of the beckoning of self-survival choices versus the duty to the eternal purpose? I wonder if you and I don't also wrestle with the god Dawn, that temptation of the *yetzer ha'ra* to return us to the "safer" life where we were in charge. Perhaps this is "veiled" mythology. The story is strange enough to be so. But there is something happening here that turns Ya'akob from one way of living to another, from mastery to

---

[29] Hamilton, V. P. (1999). 2369 שָׁחַר. In R. L. Harris, G. L. Archer, Jr. & B. K. Waltke (Eds.), *Theological Wordbook of the Old Testament*, (electronic ed.) (917). Chicago: Moody Press.

submission, from ascendency to suffering, from self-reliance to trust in the unseen God. Perhaps the story is strange because it is about more than two men fighting. Perhaps it is about *one man* fighting. Perhaps in this story we must come to terms with our own struggle to decide if we are going to be the person we have constructed or the person God has called.

What do you make of the strange request, "Let me go for ascends *hashshahar*," that is, "Let me go for the god Dawn approaches"? Is the Canaanite deity, the practice of placating to gain advantage, now left behind? Is Ya'akob finally free of his addiction to control? Perhaps the story is just too strange for us to *understand*, but it might not be too strange to *feel*.

10.

"**Then Jacob was left alone**, and a man wrestled with him until daybreak." Genesis 32:24 NASB

We have examined the trauma and family dynamics that lead to the crossing. Ya'akob's encounter on that fateful night is not a singular event but rather the culmination of several generations of divine and human preparation. What happens at Jabbok cannot be read in isolation from the transgenerational story. Now it is time to take a serious look at the event itself.

On the surface, especially in translation, the story seems straightforward. Jacob is alone. He fights all night. He is defeated but tenacious. He is blessed with a new name, Israel. But nothing about this story is so simple. Why does Jacob go back? Why is he alone? Who is this "man"? What is this fight all about? Why is there any concern about the coming dawn? How is Jacob injured? The questions just keep coming. We have examined some of these, but there are many more.

For most of us, the real question in this story is, "Who is the man?" Nahum Sarna offers a lengthy analysis of the Jewish interpretation of this story.[30] He notes that ancient myths about river gods and nighttime demons have been demythologized in this

---

[30] Cf. Nahum Sarna, *The JPS Torah Commentary: Genesis*, Excursus 24, pp. 403-404. But compare Hamilton, *Genesis*, Vol. 2, pp. 326-339 for the Christian interpretation.

71

account so that it is compatible with the monotheism of Israel. He suggests that the "man" here is the celestial patron of Esau who battles Jacob on the border of the promised land (Jabbok is the geographical separation between Mesopotamia and the Promised Land) and that, as a result of the battle, Esau's claim for the birthright is finally relinquished to Jacob (the blessing). But this seems like an odd conclusion for it is not the "man" who is defeated but rather Ya'ako<u>b</u>. Hamilton notes (as does Sarna) that Ya'ako<u>b</u> identifies the "man" as *elohim*. "The narrator's use of the term *'ish* provides another illustration of the inability of mortals to ascertain the divinity of a supernatural visitor until this visitor performs some wonder."[31] But Sarna points out that *elohim* can be used to designate God, angels and even men. The reference here is ambiguous. Only Ya'ako<u>b</u> recognizes the man's identity and only *after* the encounter. This, as we shall see, is crucially important.

We begin by looking at the language concerning the fight itself. The Hebrew verb translated "wrestled" is *'abaq*. It is spectacularly *unusual*. In fact, this story is the only place where it occurs in this form. There is another, apparently unrelated, word spelled with the same consonants but pointed differently in Song of Songs (3:6). There the word means "powder," as in the scented dust of the merchants. But maybe these two ideas, wrestling and dust, are not unrelated.

What isn't obvious in English is the origin of the

---

[31] Victor Hamilton, *Genesis*, Vol. 2, NICOT, (Eerdmans, 1995), p. 330.

Hebrew verb, "to wrestle." We need to know about its background to see the symbolism in this event. Sarna notes the word play with the name of the river (Yabboq, Ya'ako<u>b</u> and '<u>ab</u>oq).[32] He comments that some ancient Jewish scholars derived the verb from the Hebrew word "dust" or "dirt".[33] While it is a picture of what happens when two men struggle with each other in the dirt, this idea might have a bit more to say to us. Ya'ako<u>b</u>'s encounter is a face-off with who he really is. He is taken back to the very nature of his being, to the way God made him. Ya'ako<u>b</u> is the name he has made for himself, the name he has constructed out of the basic dust of his life. But here he discovers that his formation of the substance from which he came is not sufficient any more. It's time to start again. The old dust has to be reformed into some other human being. That is the wrestling match of every life. Ya'ako<u>b</u>'s wrestling might just be the tension between the man he made of the dust and the man God calls him to be from the dust.

The text employs unusual words to draw the reader into nuances. Perhaps one of those nuances isn't about an angelic stranger or a celestial patron. If wrestling is related to dust, then we are provided with a connection to the source of human being. Perhaps Ya'ako<u>b</u> is wrestling with the dust from

---

[32] In English translation, *Yabboq* becomes Jabbok, but the translation obscures the alliteration and linguistic connection between Ya'ako<u>b</u>, '<u>ab</u>oq (wrestling) and Yabboq, the river. While I will move back and forth between the English and the Hebrew, the reader should not lose sight of this important connection.

[33] Nahum Sarna, *The JPS Torah Commentary: Genesis*, footnote 10, p. 366.

which he came. There is no way to know for sure, of course. All we have is Hebrew assonance, word play and deliberate choices of unique constructions. We may have demythologized paganism. But what if this is a psychological battle (it may also be a physical one)? What if Ya'ako<u>b</u> returns to the empty side of the river because he is fighting his inner enemy, the enemy of his past life—himself? What if Ya'ako<u>b</u>'s battle is with the character he has crafted from his own origin? That would be a fight he could not win—or lose.

What is the dust of your life like? Have you formed it into an image made by your own hands? Have you taken the basic material you were born with and shaped a person who bears a resemblance to something fashioned into your idea of success? If so, there is a wrestling match ahead. Your dust will become the place of a great struggle with God. You can fight all you like, but when the dark night of the soul is over, the dust of your life will be defeated. You will have nothing left but dirt between your fingers.

At that moment, when you finally see your life as dust, you can do what Ya'ako<u>b</u> did. You can grip God with all that you have left. You can cling to Him refusing to let go. You can say, "Bless me." But be ready for a change in constitution. God will bring you to defeat. That old dust will have to be overcome before the blessing can be given. And when it is overcome, God will resurrect the basic dust of your life into what He intended it to be from the beginning.

Perhaps it is only midrash, but perhaps Ya'akob's night of struggle is also ours—each of us, alone, battling the "dust" of our origin and the shape we have made of it. Each of us, alone, pitted against where we have come from and where we are going. We have our own night demons, river gods and strange enemies to fight. We birthed them as we shaped our lives. And now, at the border to the Promised Land, we must leave them behind. We must extricate them from ourselves. We must become someone else or we cannot cross over.

My enemy just might be me.

_____

Ya'akob, the manipulator, has lived his life by his wits. Although the Bible tells us that he was a man of great strength, it is his cunning and deceit that gives him his advantage. He knows how to work a situation so that he comes out on top. His brother, his father and eventually his father-in-law are all victims of his special strength. But when he comes to the brook Yabboq, Ya'akob knows that his days of double-dealing are ending. Tomorrow he will face Esau. Powerful, able to take revenge, potentially filled with hatred, Esau approaches with four hundred men. Ya'akob knows that tomorrow he may die. So he sends his family and all of his possessions ahead. He is alone, left behind to contemplate his fate.

What do you suppose he thought and felt standing on the far side of the brook? Here's a "between the lines" possibility. Ya'akob faces the end of his identity as he knows it. His scheming and dreaming are over. All of the strength that had been so much the advantage in his life soon would be of no use. Furthermore, he is preparing himself to cross into the Promised Land. He knows that YHVH has fulfilled the promise made those many years ago, a promise that now included Ya'ako<u>b</u>'s conditions. There can be no more excuses. Ya'ako<u>b</u> is going to become someone he doesn't know because all he knows to this point is the man he has made of himself. And now he must strip himself of that man before he can enter God's land.

On this night, Ya'ako<u>b</u> wrestles with his greatest fears and his deepest trauma. Ya'ako<u>b</u> believes he is about to lose everything. He prepares for disaster. A stranger comes in that darkest moment to wrestle. They fight. Ya'ako<u>b</u> hangs on to the old ways – his strength – until the end. But Ya'ako<u>b</u> cannot win. In the final moment of collapse and failure, he cries out for favor. "I will not let go until you bless me. Even though I am beaten, even though I will die tomorrow, tonight I will not let go." As we shall see, being beaten is just the beginning.

Have you come to the end of your particular coping strengths? Have you arrived at the place where the default behavior of your life will not work anymore; where you know that tomorrow you are finished? That night you will wrestle with yourself—the tension between who you made yourself to be and the person God called you to be. You will fight to keep the old, the familiar, but you will lose. The blessing comes in tenacious defeat, not whimpering submission. In your own strength, you cannot cross the brook. You will need a new name to go on.

11.

He said, "Your name shall no longer be Jacob, but Israel; for you have striven with God and with men and have prevailed."[34] Why is Ya'akob called Yisra'el? The man in the story tells us. Yisra'el (Israel) is somehow a name that means "striving with God." Payne's comment is instructive:

> The name *yiśrā'ēl* was bestowed upon Jacob by the Angel of Yahweh (q.v.) himself, after he had wrestled with him all night (Gen 32:24 [H 25]). Jacob's struggle was spiritual, in prayer (Hos 12:4 [H 5]), as well as physical. And in it the patriarch "prevailed." Not that Jacob defeated God, but that he finally attained God's covenantal requirement of yielded submission (dramatically signalized by his injured thigh, Gen 32:25 [26]). And he persisted in refusing to let the Angel go until he had blessed him (v. 26 [H 27]). The Lord then declared, "Your name shall no longer be Jacob, *ya'ăqōb* "supplanter" (q.v.), but *yiśrā'ēl* "Israel"; for you have striven, *śārîtā* (KJV, for as a prince hast thou power, as if from the root *śar* "prince") with God and with men and have prevailed" (v. 28, NASB).[35]

A few additions are necessary. The idea that Ya'akob's struggle was spiritual and in prayer is an interpretation of the prophet Hosea. It is possible,

---

[34] Genesis 32:28 NASB

[35] Payne, J. B. (1999). 2287 שָׂרָה. In R. L. Harris, G. L. Archer, Jr. & B. K. Waltke (Eds.), *Theological Wordbook of the Old Testament* (electronic ed.) (883). Chicago: Moody Press.

of course, but the actual account doesn't say this. Payne's remark that Ya'ako<u>b</u> "attained God's covenantal requirement" is also an interpretation of the text. The story says nothing about this. In fact, the story is much more terse than the usual expansions of later theology. Payne declares that the pronouns refer to "Lord" ("the Lord declared"), but the text doesn't even say this. It is *Ya'akob*, not YHVH, who states that the encounter was with *elohim*. The narrator says only that Ya'ako<u>b</u> wrestled with a man (*'ish*). Furthermore, the statement of the contender ("Let me go for the dawn is breaking") makes almost *no sense* if the combatant is YHVH. Whatever is happening in this story, there is no doubt at all that it has become fodder for endless amplifications and midrashim.

There is also no doubt that the name Israel is related to *struggle*! That's what the "man" says. That's what the story clearly reveals. The only question is whether or not this struggle is also true of all who bear the ancestry and adoption of Ya'ako<u>b</u>. When anyone is the offspring of Ya'ako<u>b</u>, is he or she then destined for struggle?

Weiss adds an illuminating comment. "The language of the service itself [the Jewish synagogue practice] underscores the inherent assertiveness of Jewish prayer. In the petitional passage of the *Amida*, we ask for discernment (*haskel*), understanding (*bina*), and knowledge (*de'ah*)— ambitious requests by any standard. We ask that we be repeatedly forgiven (*hamarbeh lisloah*)—not just marginally excused. We ask that the arrogant among us be uprooted (*te'aker*), crushed (*teshaber*), cast down (*temager*), and humbled (*takhniya*)—not just defeated. We ask that Jerusalem be established for eternity (*binyan olam*)—not just built."[36] In other words, we declare, proclaim and insist that God do what He says He will do! We hold Him accountable. We press Him to keep His word.

This is not the kind of prayer we grew up with, but it is a needed correction to our feeble and enervated ritual. Perhaps we all need prayer with teeth. Yes, that's what's required.

If you happen to encounter a man in the middle of the night who seems intent on wrestling you to the ground, fight! And maybe you will also find a blessing—after you have been wounded for life.

---

[36] Avraham Weiss, *Holistic Prayer: A Guide to Jewish Spirituality* (Maggid, 2014), p. 55.

12.

"Please tell me your name." After Ya'ako<u>b</u> is blessed, he asks the name of his assailant. But the man doesn't answer. Instead, the man asks a very important question. "Why is it that you ask my name?" The English translation alters the Hebrew so that it fits our cultural expectations. In fact, the answer to Ya'ako<u>b</u>'s inquiry is a question that probably should be understood as, "For what *purpose* do you ask my name?" The man does not give his name. Instead he asks Ya'ako<u>b</u> (now Yisra'el) *why* he wants to know.

Why would Ya'ako<u>b</u> (Yisra'el) want to know the name of the man who blessed him?

We have investigated the power of names in Hebrew thought. To know a name is to know the character of the thing named, and in this respect, to have power over that thing. This is Ya'ako<u>b</u>'s default mechanism. If I know who you are, I know what makes you tick and consequently, I know what to do to manipulate you. To ask for a name is to ask for a revelation of self-identity. In other words, in Hebrew you are what your name says. The man does not answer Ya'ako<u>b</u>'s request because Ya'ako<u>b</u>'s question reveals the still-present character of Ya'ako<u>b</u>, the one who wishes to control. In fact, the man doesn't actually *refuse* Ya'ako<u>b</u>. He simply turns the question in on itself. He asks Ya'ako<u>b</u> to look inside and determine *why* he still wants to be in control. Ya'ako<u>b</u> has been given a new identity, but the old one is still there, in the shadows, looking for opportunities to reassert itself.

The man asks the new Yisra'el to begin changing his way of being in the world, to let go of the old way by becoming aware of its entrenched presence.

When the man gives the blessing of the name Yisra'el, he offers a definition of the character that accompanies the name.[37] "You have contended with *elohim* and with *anashim* and you have prevailed." If we examine this definition, we discover two crucial elements. The first is the play on words involved in the name itself. The verb for "to contend" is *sārâ*. Payne notes the important connection. "The verb *śārâ* limits itself to contexts which discuss the struggle of Jacob as he wrestled with the Angel of Yahweh at Peniel in Transjordan, upon his return from Mesopotamia to Canaan c. 1900 B.C. (Gen 32:24 [H 25]; Hos 12:4 [H 5]). The form in the latter passage, *wayyāśar*, might suggest a root *śûr*. But since biblical Hebrew includes no word with this meaning, it should probably be repointed to *wayyiśer*, apocopated from *yiśreh* (BDB, p. 975), the normal imperfect of *śārâ*. The importance of *śārâ* lies in its derived noun, Israel."[38] In other words, the verb and the name are essentially connected. To be Yisra'el *is to struggle with God and men.* And to prevail.

The second element is found in the verb *yakol* (to be able, to prevail, to overcome). Its primary meaning is "to be able," but in this context, it is used to

---

[37] This event is particularly interesting, as we shall see.

38 Payne, J. B. (1999). 2287 שָׂרָה. In R. L. Harris, G. L. Archer, Jr. & B. K. Waltke (Eds.), *Theological Wordbook of the Old Testament* (R. L. Harris, G. L. Archer, Jr. & B. K. Waltke, Ed.) (electronic ed.) (883). Chicago: Moody Press.

indicate that Ya'ako<u>b</u> is *not* utterly defeated. Ya'ako<u>b</u> may not be the victor but he is also not the complete loser. He has battled to the point of standoff. Neither he nor the man is the final winner.

Paul Gilchrist translates this crucial passage as "for you have striven with God and with me and have prevailed."[39] The change from "men" to "me" has interesting theological Trinitarian implications, but the meaning of Yisra'el is not left in doubt. Jonathan Sacks notes that Israel has always been a people who are constituted by their struggles to maintain self-identity.[40] The entire story is a tale about self-identity.

Sacks points out that Ya'ako<u>b</u>'s actions prior to Jabbok were the actions of a son who "wanted to be his brother."[41] Perhaps we could add that prior to Yabboq this man's life is determined by the meaning provided by someone else. It may be that Ya'ako<u>b</u> desired Esau's place as first-born, but Ya'ako<u>b</u> allowed his brother to determine who he was. He lived according to the framework of his brother. At Jabbok, Ya'ako<u>b</u> learns that to be the one YHVH intended, he must recognize this self-construction as the wish to be other than who is destined to be *and* at the same time accept the destiny of YHVH's call to be the man of struggle.

---

[39] Gilchrist, P. R. (1999). 866 יָכֹל. In R. L. Harris, G. L. Archer, Jr. & B. K. Waltke (Eds.), *Theological Wordbook of the Old Testament* (R. L. Harris, G. L. Archer, Jr & B. K. Waltke, Ed.) (electronic ed.) (378). Chicago: Moody Press.

[40] Jonathan Sacks, *Radical Then, Radical Now: On Being Jewish* (Bloomsbury, 2000), pp. 196-206.

[41] Ibid., p. 197.

The man lying in the dust must now decide who he will be for himself.

Control comes to an end. Life is beyond us. When we realize this truth, we are ready to be called to a purpose beyond ourselves, a purpose that we do not control. But we do participate. This is why Ya'ako<u>b</u> neither dies nor instantly stops acting like the old Ya'ako<u>b</u>. The change in identity continues to alter who he is but it does not *erase* who he was. As long as we continue to construct our own identity based on our perceptions of who we wish to be, we will stay on the wrong side of the river, fighting with ourselves. We can only cross into the purposes God has in mind when we come to admit our limitation. Long before Yabboq, YHVH reiterated the covenant promise to Ya'ako<u>b</u>. Isaac gave the same covenant blessing to undisguised Ya'ako<u>b</u>. Now Ya'ako<u>b</u> must make that blessing a reality in his life by coming to terms with his calling, not his constructing. Now he must stop trying to be the first-born and realize God's promise has always been outside the traditions of men. God is not a man that He should conform to the ways of men. Lying in the dust at the edge of the water, Ya'ako<u>b</u> must give up his traditions in order to become human.

13.

Ya'ako<u>b</u> named the place Peniel, "Because I have seen God face-to-face, and yet my life has been preserved." [42] When Ya'ako<u>b</u> named geography, the name he chose carried a significant meaning for him. Bethel, the site of his famous dream about a stairway to heaven, means "the house of God." Peniel means "the face of God." But Ya'ako<u>b</u> had a bit more in mind than facial features when he chose this name. Ya'ako<u>b</u> chose a name that memorialized a life-altering experience, long after his first encounter with God. Much to Ya'ako<u>b</u>'s surprise, he believed that he encountered God after a lifetime of manipulation and he did not die. The gap between Bethel and Peniel is a lesson for all of us.

Ya'ako<u>b</u> became a manipulator, a schemer and a self-made man. He spent his days looking for the angles. Sometimes "fate" seemed to play the same tricks on him. He wound up in bed with the wrong wife. But even that didn't stop him from getting his own way. He settled the score with Laban after years of planning. The amazing truth about Ya'ako<u>b</u>'s lifestyle is that he acted as though his first encounter with God had no effect on his behavior. At Bethel, God promised Ya'ako<u>b</u> protection and blessing. But Ya'ako<u>b</u> ran his own ship for many years after that encounter. His sexual behavior is probably the clearest example of the odd interplay between self-indulgence and divine

---

[42] Genesis 32:30 NASB

87

purpose. With four partners producing thirteen children, the family dynamics must have been filled with tension. The story provides several hints about the rivalry and animosity in the family. Consider Leah's constant dismay concerning not being loved or the interplay between the sisters when they debate who will sleep with their husband (Genesis 30:15). The fact that Ya'ako<u>b</u> shows no resistance to multiple partners certainly demonstrates his intention to control the situation as best as he can. It may be true that the culture did not frown on a man with multiple females but that does not mean YHVH's original instruction regarding monogamy was inapplicable. Perhaps the strangest result of Ya'ako<u>b</u>'s sexual activities is that YHVH used these circumstances to bring about the twelve tribes. It seems that most of Ya'ako<u>b</u>'s life is God's instructions mixed with Ya'ako<u>b</u>'s alterations.

One day YHVH came to Ya'ako<u>b</u> with the command, "Return to the land of your fathers." The verb is *shuv*, a verb that is commonly used to describe repentance and return to YHVH. Of course, it is also a word that describes physical return, but the multiple meanings may be included in YHVH's instruction. YHVH may be saying, "Your time is finished. It is now time to come back to Me." So Ya'ako<u>b</u> prepares for the return and when he is at the last step before entering the Promised Land, he meets the man at the brook.

In the darkest time in his life, the day before he would face the brother he had cheated, he encounters a foe he cannot beat. Ya'ako<u>b</u> experiences defeat and despair. The next day, exhausted, he would have to look into the face of

Esau. Ya'ako<u>b</u> realizes that the fateful judgment day has come. He is at the bottom of the pit. Now where is God's protection and favor?

Something happened to Ya'ako<u>b</u> when he finally faced himself, when he realized he could not get the advantage. In spite of his defeat, Ya'ako<u>b</u> clung to this man and refused to let go until he received a blessing from his conqueror. And what blessing did he get? He was probably looking for a blessing of strength to face Esau. But what he got was a new name. How he got the name is the fulcrum of this story.

The victor, this strange man of the night, asks Ya'ako<u>b</u>, "What is your name?" The Hebrew text is slightly different. *Mash-shemeka*—an idiomatic expression that could be translated, "What name is yours?" The man isn't asking Ya'ako<u>b</u> for the word on his birth certificate. He is asking how Ya'ako<u>b</u> *identifies himself.* In Semitic parlance, he is asking Ya'ako<u>b</u> to say the word that speaks about how he views his own self-consciousness. "Who are you?" asks the man. That is, what word will you provide to describe the person that you have become. And Ya'ako<u>b</u> answers with his name, the name that has been associated with his deception, manipulation and control. The name given to him by someone else. He might as well have said, "I am the deceiver, the supplanter, the master of my fate. This is what everyone calls me."

"Your name shall no longer be Ya'ako<u>b</u>, but Yisra'el." Pay close attention to the sematic construction. It is literally, "Not Ya'ako<u>b</u> shall be spoken again." The negative is the stronger of the

89

two Hebrew options. *Lo* means "without condition," the absolute negative, as opposed to *'al*, the negative that applies under certain circumstances. This man states unequivocally that the summation of the character found in the name Ya'ako<u>b</u> will no longer apply. The verb in this phrase is *'amar*. It means, "to say, to speak, to say to oneself, to think, to command, to promise." It is the common Hebrew verb for speech. From this point onward, the person who used to be Ya'ako<u>b</u> will no longer be identified by the meaning of *ya'ako<u>b</u>*. He will not speak as Ya'ako<u>b</u>. He will not think as Ya'ako<u>b</u>. He will not understand himself as Ya'ako<u>b</u>. From this point onward, he will be identified as Yisra'el, the one who contended with both God and men and prevailed.

The definition of the name Ya'ako<u>b</u> was provided by Esau. Esau was the one who attached "deceiver" to the name. Nevertheless, Ya'ako<u>b</u> lived up to this definition. He allowed someone else to tell him who he was. Now the "man" gives a new definition to a new name. Once again someone else provides the meaning of Ya'ako<u>b</u>'s life (now Yisra'el's life). The rest of the story is the interplay between these two names. It is the saga of Ya'ako<u>b</u> learning how to become Yisra'el. It is the psychological drama of determining the meaning of my name *myself*! This man must now determine who he is. He has been released from his past and the name associated with his past, but it is not erased. For the rest of his life, he will have to contend with the struggle to determine his own identity.

Yisra'el has a new name that no longer meant what he had made of his former name. He received a blessing he did not expect. When Ya'akob wrestled in the dark, his identity changed. Defeated, he was forced to admit who he saw himself to be. He was the person who let others define his name. He was the one who made himself into the supplanter. His life was a testimony to changing "the one who comes after" into "the one who comes out on top." Then he met someone who could not be manipulated and all of the meaning he attempted to make of *ya'akob* meant nothing.

"I admit that I am powerless over what I have made of myself—that my life has become unmanageable."

If you are wrestling with God in the dark, you're in the right place for a name change. Perhaps Moses reflected on Ya'akob's encounter when he wrote, "He found him in a desert land, and in the howling waste of a wilderness; He encircled him, He cared for him, He guarded him as the pupil of His eye" (Deuteronomy 32:10). Have you ever been in the wilderness at night? Far from the man-made delusions of protective cities, scary things move in the dark. Once in awhile you can see eyes just outside your psychological protection. But you will never be more frightened than when you hear the howl. The cry of an animal brings all of our insufficiency into focus. It is the cry that confirms we don't belong in this place.

Howling (*yelel*) is connected with *tohu*, a word that gives us an even more disturbing picture. *Tohu* is the word for chaos, confusion and meaninglessness. You will find it in Genesis 1:2

("without form"). It is primeval disorder. There is something sinister about this kind of existence. And if you look deeply enough into your own soul, you will find just this kind of place; a place where the malevolent beast within howls its cry of destruction.

God finds us in just this place. At the end of ourselves, confused, disordered, frightened, feeling the claws of our own inner destruction pawing at the inside, screaming to get out. This is the real desert—the emptiness that knows no boundaries. Inner space. This is the place where God rescues me because no one else can, not even my own soul. I hear my own unutterable cry of terror and discover that it is not too much for God to listen to. Everything in me wants to run away, until God puts His hand on my shoulder and whispers those words I have longed to hear in my howling waste: "I will protect you." This is the place where I am given permission to determine my own name.

If you have never been to the howling waste, you are either blessed or cursed. If you have never been there because God spared you from knowing the depth of your desperation, you are blessed. But if you have never been there because you have been running for protection ever since you heard that first howl, you are pitifully cursed. The howl will never end until it encounters the God who lives in the waste places. Until the word of God comes in the desert, the howl holds us in fear. If you hear the silence howling, stop running. God knows that sound too.

In waste places God can give you freedom to

change who you made yourself to be. He can give you permission to take a new name—a name not determined by what others have told you. A new name that you can become.

14.

Jacob lifted up his eyes. The battle in the night is over. Esau approaches. But it is still Ya'akob who meets him. In fact, the interplay between Ya'akob and Yisra'el continues through the rest of Genesis. But things have changed.

Ya'akob is the man who interacts with Esau, finally reconciling after years of bitterness and fear. Ya'akob is the father who does not act at Shechem and who experiences trouble as a result of his sons' deception. Ya'akob is the man whom God visits at Bethel. Ya'akob is the husband who loses his beloved Rachel. Ya'akob is the man who buries his father Isaac. Ya'akob is the man who moved away from his brother. Ya'akob is the father who agonizes over the news of the death of his son Joseph. Ya'akob is the patriarch who suffers through the famine. Ya'akob is the father who fears the loss of Simeon and Benjamin. Ya'akob is the man whose hope is revived about his lost sons. Ya'akob is the priest who blesses Pharaoh. Ya'akob is the grandfather who reverses the blessing to his grandsons. Ya'akob is the dying man who speaks to the character and destiny of his sons. Ya'akob is the one who is gathered to his kin after a long life tossed between despair and joy.

Yisra'el is another story. Yisra'el is the man whom YHVH blesses at Paddan-aram, repeating the change in character-name that Ya'akob received from the man at Jabbok. Yisra'el is the man who journeyed beyond the grave of Rachel. Yisra'el is the head of the household whom Reuben attempts to overthrow. Yisra'el is the name by which the sons are known. Yisra'el is the man of deep love for Joseph. Yisra'el is the authority that Joseph obeys. Yisra'el is the man who relinquishes his fear about Benjamin. Yisra'el is the one who experiences the joy of discovering Joseph is alive. Yisra'el is the old man who requests a vow from his son. Yisra'el is the one who blesses Manasseh and Ephraim. Yisra'el is the patriarch who distinguishes between the identity of his sons from the world's point-of-view and his own understanding of them. And Yisra'el is the one who is buried in Canaan.

Genesis 46:2 demonstrates how intertwined the two names become. "God spoke to Israel in visions of the night and said, 'Jacob, Jacob.' And he said, 'Here I am.'" YHVH comes to the man of destiny—Yisra'el. But He addresses him as the man of submission—Ya'ako<u>b</u>. And it is Ya'ako<u>b</u> who answers, who accepts his past and declares his affiliation with his grandfather, Abraham, with the Hebrew "*Hinneni*." Ya'ako<u>b</u>-Yisra'el is never one or the other. He is both. One he constructed that he has now relinquished. One he has been given that he now accepts. But he cannot be who he is without both identities. Both identities continue to be expressed for the remainder of his life. The tension between them is permanent. The *yetzer ha'ra*, that instinctual force of survival that expands to all facets of living, has been subdued. The *yetzer ha'tov* directs, bending the *yetzer ha'ra* to the service of eternal purposes. But the *yetzer ha'ra* doesn't go away. In fact, it *cannot* go away because this man exists in the tension between his own construction and God's calling. He is what others call him *and* what God asks of him.

After Yabboq, Ya'akob experiences the consequences of a self-made identity. He has an uneasy peace with his brother. He buries those he loved. He feels the agony of loss. He suffers both physically and emotionally. He faces deception from his own sons. He longs for hope. And he recognizes the impact of his own life on the destinies of his sons.

After Yabboq, Yisra'el encounters the loving care of God. He goes beyond sorrow. He establishes a name that has eternal purpose. He learns to trust YHVH. He takes on the role of priest. He changes the fate of tradition. He knows peace.

Crossing Yabboq is the turning point in the life of this man—self-made, filled with unmet emotional needs, striving to control the world of threat—he is also the man of God's calling—eternally focused, identified with the divine, ready to accept life as it is.

Moses asks for a sign and the sign God gives is something that can occur only *after* Moses has completed what God asks. Ya'akob is the one who will carry forth the covenant promise to Abraham but he can do so only *after* he relinquishes his control over how the promise will be fulfilled. God's hand is operating all the time even when we can't see it. Ya'akob acknowledges this. "God was in this place and I did not know it." But this is true of *all* of Ya'akob's life. In the first part of his life, Ya'akob holds on to a psychological frontier of survival. He takes care of himself. But this kind of survival means not surrendering to the will of another. It means staying in control. The *yetzer ha'ra* is vital at the beginning. It is the power to keep us alive. But as we grow, so does the demand of the *yetzer ha'ra* and whatever appears as a threat to its control is converted into a threat to *survival* until at last we are operating in the fullest extent of *self-sufficiency.* This is what God confronts. This is what we must battle, and what will ultimately *defeat* us because it is not possible to live and at the same time erase the will to survive. But it is possible. In fact, it is necessary to surrender the power to the One who gives life.

The serpent provides H̱avvah with the opportunity to survive without surrender. Ya'akob̲ is confronted at Yabboq with the consequences of survival without surrender. He learns to change. So can we.

"Freedom is the liberation from the tyranny of the self-centered ego. It comes about in moments of transcending the self as an act of spiritual ecstasy, of stepping out of the confining framework of routine reflexive concern. Freedom presupposes *the capacity for sacrifice.*"[43]

---

[43] Abraham Heschel, "Religion in a Free Society" in *The Insecurity of Freedom: Essays on Human Existence* (The Noonday Press, 1967), p. 15.

Crossing Over Self-helplessness

I'm sick and tired. Mostly tired. Tired of feeling the shame, the guilt. Tired of being afraid. But up to this point, not tired enough. The hypocrisy is killing me. I know it, but I can't pull myself out of the mire.

Then something happens. Suddenly I'm swept up in something spiritual, something I didn't plan. Something I actually fought against, telling myself it could never happen to me. But it did. Suddenly I'm overwhelmed by a sense of wholeness, of forgiveness, freedom from all the emotional baggage that kept me trapped in endless cycles of anger, remorse and anesthetic behavior. For reasons I can't explain, because there is no reason to it at all, those old ways of dealing with my shame evaporate. I see them for what they truly were—useless avoidance.

There is a new reality. Hope? No, I've known what it is to hope. I always hoped that change was really possible. But this it is more than hope. Hope is the anxious desire for different, but this isn't an anxious desire. This is a collection of choices that wouldn't have been possible before. It is a present reality, evidence I never thought could be mine. But there it is. I'm not the same. Not the same old same old. Days of clarity. Decisions *not* to be sick. The ability to unpack the suitcase of emotions I have been carrying all my life.

If I try to analyze the difference, I can't find any reason why. It just is. Maybe it's the hand of the unseen God at work. Maybe it's a miracle. Just a tiny, personal one that no one else sees. Maybe my dogmatic belief in the law of cause and effect needs to be shaken. Cause and effect kept me sick and suffering. Maybe there are things in the world that just are, forces without causes that crash over us like tidal waves and change who we have been into who we will be.

Maybe I just crossed over to the real world.

Skip Moen is the author of

Spiritual Restoration, Vols. 1-3

Guardian Angel

The Lucky Life

Cross Word Puzzles

God, Time and the Limits of Omniscience

Jesus Said to Her

31: Days of Transformation

He has written thousands of word studies of the biblical vocabulary.

skipmoen.com